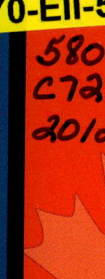

1940s

Written By
Rennay Craats

Published by Weigl Educational Publishers Limited
6325 – 10 Street SE
Calgary, Alberta, Canada
T2H 2Z9

Website: www.weigl.ca
Copyright © 2012 WEIGL EDUCATIONAL PUBLISHERS LIMITED
All rights reserved. No part of this publication may be reproduced, stored in a retrieval system, or transmitted in any form or by any means, electronic, mechanical, photocopying, recording, or otherwise, without the prior written permission of Weigl Educational Publishers Limited.

Library and Archives Canada Cataloguing in Publication

Craats, Rennay, 1973-
      1940 / Rennay Craats.

(Canadian decades)
Includes index.
ISBN 978-1-77071-714-5 (bound).--ISBN 978-1-77071-725-1 (pbk.)

     1. Canada--History--1939-1945--Juvenile literature.
2. Canada--History--1945-1963--Juvenile literature. 3. Nineteen forties--Juvenile literature. 4. Canada--Miscellanea--Juvenile literature.
I. Title. II. Series: Canadian decades

FC580.C69 2011   j971.063   C2011-904756-X

082011
WEP040711

Project Coordinator: Heather Kissock
Art Director: Terry Paulhus

Printed and bound in the United States of America, in North Mankato, Minnesota
1 2 3 4 5 6 7 8 9 0   15 14 13 12 11

Photograph Credits

Canadian Press Images: pages 9L, 12; Getty Images: pages 9 MR, 10, 11T, 11BL, 13T, 14, 15, 16, 17, 18, 19, 20, 21B, 22T, 23T, 23BR, 27L, 28, 29B, 30, 31, 32, 33, 34, 37T, 39, 40, 41T, 41L, 43; Glenbow Museum Archive: page 38; Montreal Neurological Institute: page 27B; National Archives of Canada: page 13B, 26, 36, 37B.

Every reasonable effort has been made to trace ownership and to obtain permission to reprint copyright material. The publishers would be pleased to have any errors or omissions brought to their attention so that they may be corrected in subsequent printings.

We acknowledge the financial support of the Government of Canada through the Canada Book Fund for our publishing activities.

Canadian Decades

1940s

CONTENTS

Introduction	4
Time Line	6
Disasters	8
Entertainment	10
Trends	14
World Events	16
Political Issues	20
Literature	24
Science and Technology	26
Sports	28
Economy	32
Fashion	34
Immigration	36
Music and the Arts	38
Society	40
Canada/U.S. Relations	42
Activities	44
Glossary	46
Learning More	47
Index	48

Introduction

In the 1940s, Canadians relied on the printed word in newspapers and on the crackly voice of radio announcers to inform them of local, national, and world events. Canadian Decades: The 1940s explores the events that made an impact on Canadian lives. Many of these stories made national headlines and affected Canadians for many years. Other stories faded from memory. All, however, were important to Canadian life and history.

World War II dominated the events of the 1940s. Canadians spent half of the decade fighting in Europe. Political decisions were made, and laws were passed because of the war. Women marched out of the home and into the workplace to replace the absent men, and many decided they wanted

permanent jobs. Canadians gave up coffee and tea, and cut back on meat and gasoline to support the cause. Japanese Canadians were forced into internment camps because some people feared a Japanese attack.

Many Canadian events were products of the world war, but other events and people also made an impact on society during that time. This is just one book, however, and everything that happened in the 1940s cannot be included within its pages. This volume touches on some of the important issues, people, and events that contributed to Canadian history and identity.

Canadian Decades 1940s   5

Canadian Decades 1940s

1940
A new law banning American comic books is passed in 1940. Find out how the comic hero Johnny Canuck comes to the rescue. (Page 13)

1941
The "Voice of Doom" gives Canadians information about the war on CBC's own news service. (Page 12)

1942
In 1942, the world is introduced to Frank Sinatra as a solo act. (Page 39)

1942
Canadians afraid of a Japanese attack respond by sending Japanese Canadians to internment camps. (Page 20)

1943
Count Fleet crosses the finish line first in 1943. Johnny Longden is not far behind. (Page 31)

1943
The Canadian government sets up Unemployment Insurance. (Page 32)

1943
Canadians see the war in a new way in 1943—on canvas. (Page 13)

1944
Prime Minister King makes an important decision in 1944. (Page 21)

1945
Fifty nations come together to try to prevent future wars. (Page 19).

1945
The nature of war changes forever in 1945. Japan is devastated by a new and dangerous weapon. (Page 17)

1945
Many people celebrate in 1945, as the Axis powers are finally stopped. (Page 17)

1945
Hugh MacLennan is not lonely in his solitude. His novel Two Solitudes forges a new era in Canadian literature. (Page 25)

1946
Canadians turn away from radio in 1946. (Page 15)

1946
Thousands of women board ships with their children headed for Canada. They are meeting their husbands in a new country. (Page 41)

1946
Baseball brings races together in 1946, and Montreal is part of it. (Page 28)

1947
Canadians' hopes rest on the thin blades of a figure skater. (Page 30)

1947
Dugald, Manitoba, makes headlines. This quiet town is host to a head-on train wreck at the station. (Page 9)

1947
The "New Look" invades Canada. After a war full of invasions, this one is welcome. (Page 35)

1948
The Treasure of Sierra Madre is a treasure indeed. (Page 11)

1948
In 1948, Israel is given independence from Britain, but the transition is far from smooth. (Page 19)

Canadian Decades 1940s

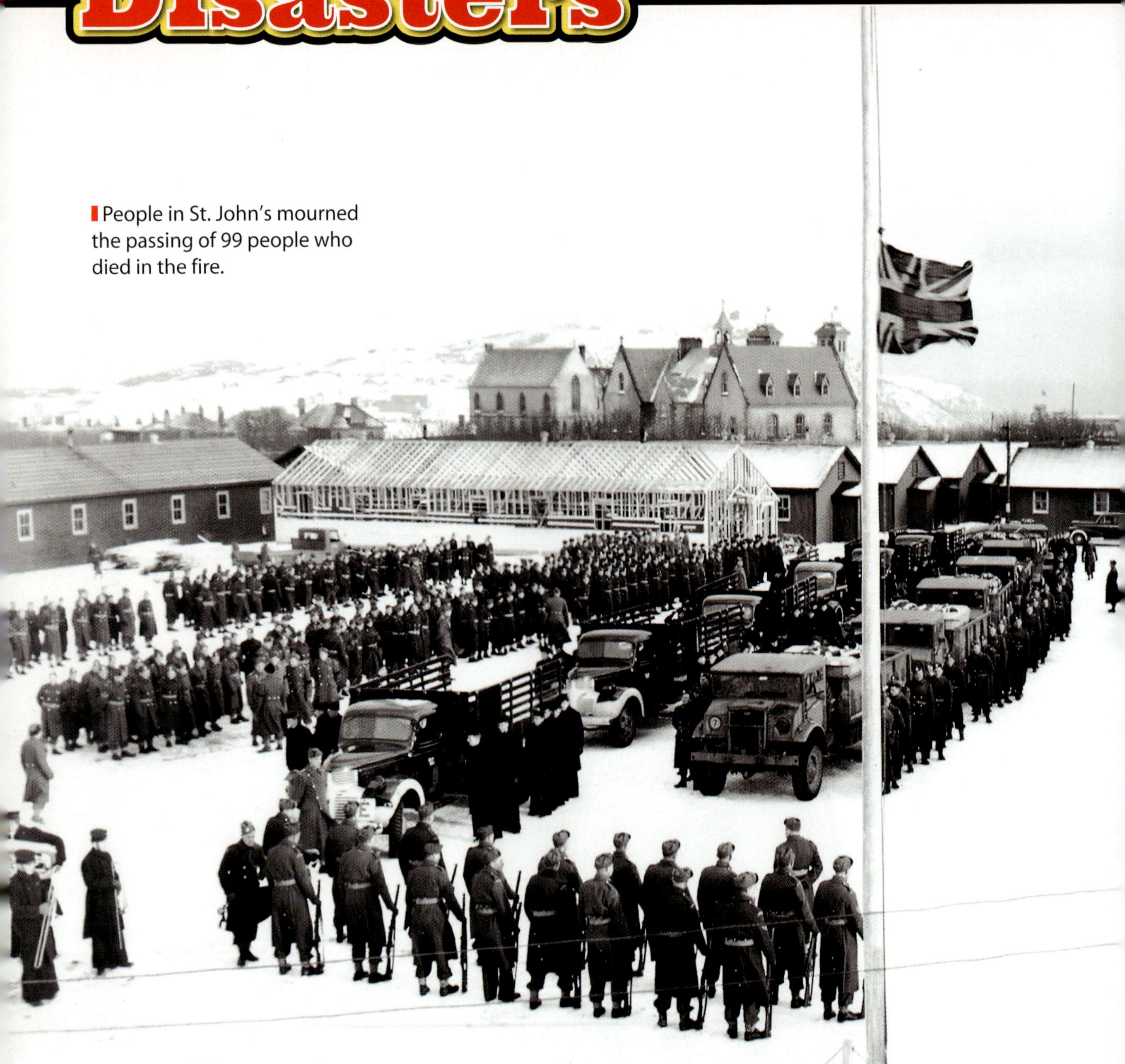

Disasters

> People in St. John's mourned the passing of 99 people who died in the fire.

Fire in St. John's

The most deadly structural fire in Canadian history occurred at the Knights of Columbus hostel in St. John's, Newfoundland. On December 12, 1942, the wartime social club was packed with military personnel and their friends. A fire broke out. There were no emergency lights, so confusion set in when the lights went out. People rushed to the exits to escape but could not pull the doors open—they were pushed against the doors by people coming behind them. The main fire hall was only 180 metres away, but the building was beyond saving before the engines even arrived. Ninety-nine people died, and another 100 were injured. It was discovered that an **arsonist** caused the fire by lighting toilet paper rolls. The fire was blamed on an enemy terrorist—no one wanted to admit that a Canadian could have set the fire. No one was arrested for this crime.

Falling from the Sky

Airplanes crash for many reasons. Sometimes, people make planes crash. This was the case on September 9, 1949. A Quebec Airways DC-3 airplane exploded. It crashed to the ground near St-Joachim, Quebec. Twenty-three people died. Investigators found that the airplane crash was not an accident. It was **sabotage**. People had purposely bombed the plane. Three men were convicted of the crime and hanged.

Sometimes, planes just crash on their own or because of a pilot error. The worst crash in the Royal Canadian Air Force's history, excluding war missions, occurred on October 19, 1943. A Liberator bomber was carrying soldiers on leave from the war. It crashed in a Quebec wilderness area. Twenty-four servicemen were killed. The wreckage of the plane was not found for nearly three years after the accident.

Polio Strikes North America and Europe

Polio epidemics caused panic and fear in the 1940s. Polio is a disease caused by a **virus**. It causes paralysis, or loss of muscle use, and nerve damage. This can rarely be reversed. The disease struck quickly, and there was no cure. Victims, mostly children, spent time on crutches or in wheelchairs, or lying in "iron lungs"—metal cylinders that helped the victims breathe.

Research for a **vaccine** had been under way at Connaught Medical Research Laboratories at the University of Toronto since 1947. American Dr. Jonas Salk, encouraged by the work being done in Toronto, created a vaccine. Connaught was asked to make large quantities of Salk's vaccine for a trial in 1953. Canadian children received the immunization in 1954. Canadian researchers then went on to help control the spread of the disease around the world.

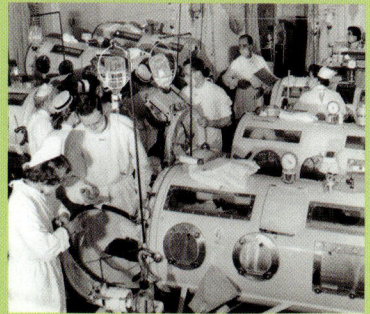

▌An iron lung forces a person's lungs to inhale and exhale through regulated changes in air pressure.

▌Dr. Salk administered polio vaccines to help children and adults alike fight off the disease.

Trains Hit Head-on

On September 1, 1947, an east-bound train pulled into Dugald, Manitoba, 30 kilometres east of Winnipeg. It was taking on additional passengers returning from their Labour Day holidays. A west-bound train came barrelling into the station at more than 50 kilometres per hour. The two trains collided head-on. The trains stood straight up on the tracks. The back cars were pulled from the rail. The impact threw the more than 1,000 passengers around, and a fire broke out. Passengers were trapped. The fire, which was caused by lamps in the rail cars, spread quickly through the mostly wooden cars. Two servicemen helped pull people from the trains until the heat became too great for them to continue. A grain elevator near the station also caught fire and burned to the ground.

Emergency crews flocked to the area. There were hundreds of vehicles parked near the crash site. Some people were there offering help. Others were straining to watch the disaster. Doctors and medical supplies were flown into Dugald. The planes then carried seriously injured people to the hospital. Thirty-one people died in the accident.

> "A bolt of fire, like an electric flash, came right through the car and then the car caught on fire. I don't know how we got out the window, but we did."
> —A shaken passenger

Canadian Decades 1940s   9

Entertainment

Deanna Durbin— Hollywood Sweetheart

Born in Winnipeg, Manitoba, Edna Mae Durbin took singing lessons at the age of eleven. She was soon discovered by a talent agent. Within a few years, teenage Edna Mae captured the attention and adoration of the movie industry as a singing star. She appeared in a short film called Every Sunday with Judy Garland. Then Edna Mae changed her name to Deanna Durbin. The new name came with sudden new fame.

There was a flurry of movie roles, many of which focussed on her youth and innocence. In *First Love* in 1939, Durbin had her first screen kiss. The roles that followed became more and more grown-up. *Spring Parade* in 1940 was Durbin's eighth straight hit movie. The 1941 hit *It Started With Eve* was the first in which Durbin played an independent, mature woman. She filmed around fifteen other movies in the 1940s alone. In 1950, Deanna Durbin released her last movie and retired from show business.

▌By age 21, Deanna Durbin was the highest-paid female film star in the world.

Walter Huston Wows Academy

Toronto-born actor Walter Huston moved to the United States when he was 18 years old. He wanted to be a star. He acted in stage plays and **vaudeville** dramas. In 1929, he moved to Hollywood to make it big. His dreams of fame came true. He appeared in memorable Hollywood films such as *The Maltese Falcon* in 1941 and *And Then There Were None* in 1945.

He appeared on the screen with Humphrey Bogart as well as with his own son, John Huston. His most noted role was in *The Treasure of Sierra Madre* in 1948. This film had all the elements of a successful movie—panning for gold, greed, and bandits. It was nominated for four Academy Awards. Walter Huston won an Oscar for Best Supporting Actor, and John Huston won a Best Director Oscar for the movie.

Movies Help War Effort

The popularity of movies was used to encourage support of the war. **Newsreels** that showed events filmed by soldiers were played before motion pictures. The movies, most of which were made in the United States and Britain, did more than just entertain Canadians. They made them feel more **patriotic**. Many movies were about families keeping the home front running while soldiers were overseas. Movies about war service and successful military operations were very common.

The National Film Board (NFB) was created in 1939. It wanted to balance the Hollywood images of war in film. Canadian filmmakers set out to show Canada in the war. The NFB became internationally known for **propaganda** films during the 1940s. Films including *Canada Carries On*, a series released once a month, and *World in Action*, produced between 1942 and 1945, brought war messages to Canadians.

Canadians were also bombarded by other forms of propaganda. Posters, radio, film, and newspaper pieces were aimed at convincing them how positive the war was, and how important Canada was in the success of the war.

Tuning In

Families huddled around their radios listening to a popular form of entertainment in the 1940s—radio plays. During the 1947–48 season, Canadian Broadcasting Corporation (CBC) radio aired 320 radio dramas, written mostly by Canadians. In addition to dramas, CBC produced several radio shows that Canadians listened to without fail. One of the most popular programs was *The Happy Gang*. Introduced during the Great Depression, it provided a laugh in hard times. The show's theme song was the "Beer Barrel Polka," but at that time, Canadians could not say "beer" on the radio. Announcers could never say the title on the air. The show began with a knock at the door. When asked who was there, the group response was "It's the Happy Gang!" CBC also produced quality children's programming. Mary Grannan created *Just Mary*—humorous fantasy stories for Canadian children. *The Adventures of Maggie Muggins* was a favourite. This long-running radio program gave rise to a book in 1942. Grannan released *Just Mary Stories* so that parents could read the stories to their children.

Newsreels and documentaries were released to show Canadians at home what their soldiers were doing overseas.

Entertainment

After *Bonanza*, Lorne Greene went on to star in many popular television shows, including *Battlestar Galactica* and *Code Red*. He died in 1987.

The Voice of CBC

Early in World War II, the Canadian Press brought news from the war to Canada. In 1941, CBC created its own news service to receive word from war **correspondents** about what was happening. The service quickly earned a reputation for being a fair and reliable information source. The news stories were first read by Charles Jennings and then by Lorne Greene. Greene was called the "Voice of Doom." He received this nickname because of his dramatic way of telling the often bad news from the war front. After the war, Greene founded the Jupiter Theatre in Toronto, and he established and taught at the Academy of Radio Arts. In 1959, he began playing the part of Ben Cartwright on the successful American television program *Bonanza*. He played that role for 14 years. He also focussed his attention on environmental issues and wildlife preservation.

Canadian Stage Radio Plays

Andrew Allan knew the importance of radio to Canadians. He saw radio as the national theatre. He decided to make that theatre the best possible. In 1942, Allan began working at CBC in Vancouver, and then moved to Toronto. Between 1944 and 1956, Allan produced the Canadian Stage Series. This project included more than 400 plays on the radio. Some plays had already been produced, while others were original creations. Many of the dramas were written by Canadian writers. This gave these writers, including Lister Sinclair and Mavor Moore, an audience. The scripts were written for and performed by budding stars, including Lorne Greene, Jane Mallett, and John Drainie. Andrew Allan left radio to attempt to create the same magic on television. He could not bring his talents and passion across to television as well as he had on radio. He retired in 1962.

> "[Canadian Stage] gave many of us our first hint that there were Canadian writers who had something interesting to say."
> —Robert Fulford, Canadian writer

Canadian Comic Hero

During the 1930s, millions of 10-cent comic books were sold every month. In 1940, the War Exchange Conservation Act was enacted, stopping the flow of comic books. The Act prevented Canadians from importing anything that was not essential. This included American comic books. Canadian children went without reading *Batman* and the Canadian-created *Superman*. A Toronto publisher named Cy Bell saw to it that children were not without comic books for long.

He bought a printing press, hired an artist, and created *Johnny Canuck* in 1941. *Johnny Canuck* was the most popular comic of those created during the ban. Unlike many American heroes, Johnny did not have supernatural powers. He was a Canadian soldier waging war against Hitler. He single-handedly defeated **stereotypical** German and Japanese comic characters. *Johnny Canuck* was printed until 1946, when the restrictions on imports were relaxed. American publishers could ship comics to Canada for printing. Many Canadian printers laid off their artists, retired their comics, and began reprinting American titles.

▌The word canuck is slang for "Canadian." Hero *Johnny Canuck* represented Canadians in their conflict against Nazi Germany.

Artists Paint Picture of the War

In 1943, Canadian forces used artists to show the war effort. Artists painted images of recruitment, battle, wounded soldiers recovering in the hospital, and the burial of fallen soldiers. Charles Comfort was a painter and teacher at the University of Toronto. He chose the first group of artists to perform this function. He accompanied them overseas and painted portraits of Canadian soldiers. The artists wore the same uniforms and received the same wages as regular soldiers, but they did not fight. However, not fighting did not keep the artists safe. They were caught in the middle of air raids and attacks. One artist was trapped behind enemy lines for a week before being rescued. Another's ship was sunk, and he waited for hours in an unstable lifeboat. These men were an important part of the war. They illustrated the efforts of the country's soldiers in a way that all Canadians could understand. The art was later brought home for viewing. The artists provided a unique record of the war.

Canadian Decades 1940s 13

Trends

▪ *Casablanca*, starring Humphrey Bogart and Ingrid Bergman, was a favourite 1940s film.

The Silver Screen

People looked to movie screens to escape the war. People flocked to theatres to watch films. Movies cost patrons less than 50 cents to get in the door, and while they were there, they could be entertained. They could watch other people conquering the war without having to do so themselves. Even more appealing were plots that were a bit more removed from the actual fighting. They could "Play it Again" and again with the cast of *Casablanca*.

▮ The jitterbug was often danced to big-band swing music. The high-energy, fast steps kept people dancing the night away.

Dancing Their Cares Away

The forties were full of hard times. Canadians looked to big bands and dance halls to lift their spirits. A dance craze called the jitterbug helped chase away the gloom of war and keep people lively and happy. This swing dance was energetic and fun. Couples were breathless from the fast-paced dancing. The moves were difficult to follow and different from one dancer to the next. Many of the musicians who played the music could not define what the jitterbug was, or even describe the steps. A night out jitterbugging kept Canadians' feet tapping and their minds off the war for the evening.

Television-Watchers

By 1946, the days of the radio drama were numbered. The CBC was being pressured to bring television to Canadians. CBC directors wanted to act slowly and carefully—television was expensive, and they did not want to broadcast terrible shows just to provide television.

A report on television in 1947 convinced CBC to act. The report was prepared by CBC's chief engineer, J. Alphonse Ouimet, who had tried to set up a television broadcasting system in Montreal in the early 1930s. People awaited what Americans had enjoyed for years—television. The possibilities of television changed many things in Canada. Radio was restructured, and recreational time would be spent differently. It took CBC until 1952 to begin broadcasting television to eager Canadians.

Revolutionary Records

The forties welcomed many improvements in music and music-playing devices. In 1948, the concept of the LP record was released to the public. LP stands for long-playing. It was a disc with tiny grooves that wound into the centre of the record. It played at 33 1/3 revolutions per minute, or rpms.

This record spun more slowly than other records. Slower spinning meant more music could be put on one record. LPs played for 23 minutes on each side. The quality was far better than previous phonograph records. Several songs could now be recorded on a single disc.

This was great news for music lovers. Fans could now buy recordings of their favourite musicians and play an LP at home without losing quality. They could also listen without having to change the disc every few minutes. LPs became incredibly popular and remained popular into the 1970s.

Canadian Decades 1940s 15

World Events

Hitler ruled as dictator from 1933 to 1945. His personality and public speaking ability convinced people to support his Nazi leadership.

The World at War

World War II began in 1939 when Germany attacked other European countries. Unlike World War I, there was no excitement about going to war. People knew what to expect. Fighting the **Axis powers**—Germany, Italy and Japan—was something that needed to be done.

Nazi forces swept through Europe. They started the **Holocaust**. Germany's leader, Adolf Hitler, wanted to create a "master race" made up of white people. To do this, he tried to destroy those he considered inferior—mainly Jewish people. German troops forced Jewish people from their homes, took their belongings, and sent them to **concentration camps**. Italy's Benito Mussolini also ordered mass-murder in his advances. He set up concentration camps that killed thousands of Ethiopians after his forces invaded their country. He declared war against Greece and France and took over Albania, all with great violence. During the Axis powers' advance, millions of people were tortured, starved, beaten, and killed in camps. It was only after the war that the horrible truth about the camps came to light.

16 World Events

Allies Stop Hitler

After months of special training, 300,000 American, British, and Canadian troops, backed by 4,000 ships and 11,000 aircraft, set out to stop the Germans. On June 6, 1944, the **Allies** landed in Normandy for "Operation Overlord." It would soon be known as D-Day. They attacked the German **stronghold** from the air, land, and sea. By the end of the day, the Allies had not done all they had hoped, but they had re-entered Europe. The cost of the attack was high. There were 1,074 Canadians injured, 359 of whom would die. Yet their job was not complete. There would be another 11 months of intense fighting before the war in Europe was over.

By April 1945, German forces had been defeated. Adolf Hitler, surrounded by Russian troops, committed suicide. The German surrender was made official one week later, and it was signed on May 7. Millions of people celebrated the victory in Europe. Allied forces knew that they still had to end the war with Japan.

Canada at War

Canada joined the war effort in 1939. By the summer of 1939, France had fallen to the Germans, and Britain was threatened.

Canada's peacetime army had to be built up. At the beginning of the war, Canada had 13 ships and about 3,000 soldiers. By the end of it, there were 373 ships and more than 90,000 military personnel.

The United States was drawn into the war in 1941 after Japan attacked Pearl Harbor naval base in Hawaii.

Atomic Bombs Destroy Hiroshima and Nagasaki

The Japanese were the first to experience the horror of the atomic bomb. On August 6, 1945, an American B-52 bomber dropped the world's first atomic bomb on Hiroshima, Japan. This blast was 2,000 times more powerful than the largest bomb ever used before. Eighty thousand people died instantly. Many others suffered health problems or died from exposure to radiation, the dangerous particles produced after an atomic explosion. One third of the city of 100,000 people was destroyed. The rest was in ruins. Three days later, another larger bomb was dropped on Nagasaki, Japan. This blast destroyed the port and killed 60,000 people.

■ Hiroshima was destroyed by an atomic bomb called "Little Boy."

"We have spent $2 billion on the greatest scientific gamble in history—and won."
—American President Harry Truman after dropping the atomic bomb

The Japanese government immediately accepted the terms of its country's surrender. World War II officially ended the next day. While the Allies were the winners in title, no one really won the war. Great Britain and the United States each lost about half a million people. Canada's casualties numbered 42,000. Nearly 3 million Germans died in the fighting. The Soviet Union reported more than 7.5 million dead.

Political Issues

> "We were treated just like prisoners of war....We were allowed one card and one letter a week from our families, but those letters were all censored. I used to wonder how my family was getting along, I only heard from them occasionally."
> —An interned Japanese Canadian

Japanese Canadians Uprooted

After Japanese forces bombed Pearl Harbor in 1941, the RCMP **interned** any Japanese people who openly supported Japan. In 1942, a Japanese submarine was seen near Vancouver Island. This caused panic and anti-Japanese feeling to sweep British Columbia. Soon afterward, another 720 Japanese Canadians were confined. About 20,000 Japanese Canadians were forced to move at least 160 kilometres from the coast of British Columbia. These people were sent to isolated areas and could not do what they wanted to do. Their property was sold, and the Japanese Canadians had to start new lives in their new homes. Many of these people were Canadian-born citizens. Some felt that they were showing their Canadian patriotism by going along with the internship. But they were not thought of as patriots. They were thought of as security threats. People feared that Japanese forces would attack and Japanese Canadians would help them. The laws against the Japanese were not lifted until 1947.

Conscription Dilemma

Prime Minister W. L. Mackenzie King was faced with a decision. During World War II, he was not sure how Canadians would react to **conscription**, or forced military service. Quebec had always been against conscription. King promised Quebecers that he would not use conscription to support the war. As the war dragged on, English Canada as well as politicians began to call for conscription. By 1942, the support for conscription was strong. King decided to hold a vote. He let Canadians decide if he should be released from his conscription promise. English Canada voted 79 percent in favour of conscription. French Canada voted 72 percent against it. Bill 80 passed, however, and Prime Minister King was authorized to use conscription if the need arose.

In 1944, King used conscription, but the war ended before many of the drafted servicemen were shipped overseas.

Government Takes Away Choices

The war was thousands of kilometres away, but its effects were felt at home in Canada. On May 15, 1940, the federal government banned **communism** in Canada. The Communist Party was declared illegal. This could not ordinarily be done in a **democracy** such as Canada. It happened only because of the power of the Defence of Canada Regulations in times of war. Individual rights were given up for the greater good. As an example of this loss of freedoms, a man was put in prison for handing out anti-war literature.

The restrictions were not only political. The Jehovah's Witnesses, a religious group, were considered illegal on July 4, 1940. Their religion believes that violence is unacceptable. The beliefs of Jehovah's Witnesses would not allow for its followers to swear allegiance to any one nation. They also felt that a country's laws should not be followed if they conflicted with God's law. The government felt that this belief went against the war effort, so it banned the religion.

Confederation Complete

After the Great Depression, Newfoundland suffered an economic collapse. It asked Britain for help and became a colony again. World War II helped turn around Newfoundland's economy. Many army bases and military airports were set up there, and Newfoundland no longer needed Britain's help. A referendum was eventually held to determine the future of Newfoundland. In 1949, Newfoundland became Canada's 10th province. The decision to join Confederation, however, was not an easy one. Joseph Smallwood was an **advocate** of Confederation, and campaigned for Newfoundlanders to become Canadian. He said Newfoundland would be a better place for them and their children if it became a Canadian province. It took two separate votes before the issue was resolved. The vote to become part of Canada was won by fewer than 7,000 votes on March 31. Smallwood became premier of Newfoundland's first provincial government.

▎Joseph Smallwood helped to make Newfoundland Canada's 10th province.

Canadian Decades 1940s 21

Political Issues

"Bible Bill" Leads Alberta

William Aberhart was a radio evangelist with the nickname "Bible Bill." He was also a bright politician. He had never been interested in politics, but he wanted to do something to rebuild the West after the Depression. Aberhart modified a plan that would give every citizen $25 per month to buy necessary items. He created a political movement called the Alberta Social Credit League. Other political parties rejected his ideas, so he brought them into politics himself. Aberhart was elected premier of Alberta in 1935 with the world's first Social Credit government. The party claimed 56 of 63 seats in the legislature.

Aberhart found it difficult to keep the promises he made during the campaign. His ideas on debt collection saved some farms and homes, but his larger ideals were never brought into practice. After a major government crisis, the premier had to accept economic help from Britain. Aberhart died while still in office in 1942.

■ Aberhart was born in Ontario, but moved to Alberta to accept a position as a school principal.

Conquering the Arctic

Henry Larsen was first mate and then skipper of the schooner *St. Roch* for 20 years. Under Larsen's command, the schooner patrolled the Arctic waters, where it made history.

On June 23, 1940, the *St. Roch* left Vancouver for the Arctic. The schooner entered the Arctic through the south, which was a dangerous route. It became stuck in the ice and stayed that way over two winters. The ship did not complete its passage and arrive in Halifax until October 11, 1942. The *St. Roch* was the second ship to travel the Northwest Passage, and it was the first to make the trip from west to east. The ship made the trip back to Vancouver in only 86 days. This expedition made the *St. Roch* the first to travel the waterway both ways. These patrols strengthened Canada's claim to the Arctic. The land is Canadian, but there was dispute about whether the straits and channels belonged to Canada as well.

■ The Canadian Arctic stretches across an area of 3.5 million square kilometres.

Women Finally Have the Vote

By 1918, most Canadian women over the age of 21 could vote in federal elections. Provincial elections, however, were another matter. Between 1916 and 1925, the majority of Canadian women could vote in provincial elections. The only province that had not given women that right was Quebec. For years, women in Quebec fought to catch up with the rest of Canada. Thérèse Casgrain led the struggle, and Quebec women supported her. On April 25, 1940, the Quebec government finally granted women the right to vote in provincial elections—they had been casting their ballots for federal candidates for more than 20 years.

■ Voting is the most basic way for citizens to be involved in politics.

Spy Story Unfolds

A clerk named Igor Gouzenko worked at the Soviet Embassy in Ottawa. He learned about a Soviet network of spies trying to discover military secrets. Gouzenko **defected** to Canada in September 1945. He revealed information about this spy ring. He was not taken seriously, even though he had documents telling about Soviet spying in Canada. The Soviet embassy sent agents to Gouzenko's house to recapture him—they failed. It was only then that the government listened to what he had to say.

Prime Minister King authorized the arrest of twelve suspects named in Gouzenko's evidence. The spies were looking for information about secrets such as the atomic bomb. Several people were convicted and sent to prison for **espionage**. One of the convicted spies was Fred Rose, a member of Parliament for three years. He was found guilty of passing wartime secrets to the Soviets. He insisted he was innocent. He was sentenced to six years in jail. The spy story stunned the country.

▌When he came out of hiding, which was rare, Gouzenko wore a hood to hide his identity.

The King's Reign

William Lyon Mackenzie King was the Liberal party leader from 1921 until 1948. He served as prime minister for 22 of those years. In 1930, King refused to admit that the Great Depression was taking hold of the country. He lost the election. King stayed on as opposition leader. He brought attention to the government's broken promises and rising unemployment.

King was voted in as prime minister again in 1935. He negotiated trade agreements with the United States to help the economy. The war broke out in 1939, and King called an election. He won easily. He then addressed concerns about forced military service. He decided to send drafted troops into the war in 1944 because of high casualties and fewer volunteers. In 1940, King introduced social assistance and health insurance. These initiatives helped him narrowly win the election in 1945. He was persuaded to resign as Canada's longest-lasting leader in 1948. He died two years later.

Socialist Saskatchewan

Thomas Douglas became a politician so that he could help people. He ran for office in Saskatchewan in 1934. Douglas was not elected. He tried again as a Co-operative Commonwealth Federation (CCF) candidate in 1935. He won a seat in Parliament.

World War II made Douglas's **socialist** ideas stronger. Socialism is a system in which ownership and production is in the hands of the community and not the individual. Douglas argued that the federal government said it did not have money to put people to work but it found money for war. He said money should be spent on Canadians. Douglas resigned from his position as an MP in 1944 and competed in the Saskatchewan election.

He became premier and led the country's first socialist government for 17 years. Many of Douglas's ideas were adopted by other provinces. Saskatchewan was the first province to offer government-funded health care. Douglas resigned as premier in 1961 to lead the New Democratic Party (NDP).

▌King is considered one of Canada's most important nation builders.

Canadian Decades 1940s

Literature

Canada Sees the Wind

W.O. Mitchell was known for his writing about western Canada and the Prairies. His strength as a writer and his western settings influenced many other Prairie writers. In 1947, Mitchell released *Who Has Seen the Wind*, bringing him instant success and recognition. The novel explored the meanings of birth, death, life, freedom, and justice through a young boy named Brian. Mitchell captured the beauty of the Prairies and the power of the wind. The novel was translated into French in 1974 as well as several other languages. It was also made into a successful movie in 1977.

W.O. Mitchell wrote several radio and television plays. Many, such as *Jake and the Kid*, originated as stories in *Maclean's* magazine and ran on CBC radio. The series was made for television in 1961 and revived in the 1990s. Some of his early plays, including *The Devil's Instrument* in 1949, were later made into full-length plays. In 1973, W.O. Mitchell became a Member of the Order of Canada.

Under the Volcano

Many people argue that Malcolm Lowry's *Under the Volcano* is one of the best novels in modern literature. Although not born in Canada, Lowry spent much of his time in British Columbia. Much of his fiction was set in that province. Most of his fiction was at least a little **autobiographical**. *Under the Volcano* is no exception. He based the book on his experiences in Mexico.

The novel was the product of 10 years of writing and rewriting. He applied the finishing touches on Christmas Eve, 1944, but it took years before the public would read it. *Under the Volcano* was accepted for publication in 1946 and was finally published in 1947. He wrote other novels, including *Lunar Caustic*. His final novel, *October Ferry*, was published in 1970, long after his death.

Emily Carr's Many Talents

Emily Carr spent her life being creative. She painted the Aboriginal communities in British Columbia, trying to provide a record of their disappearing culture and villages. In 1927, Carr met the Group of Seven, a group of artists who often painted landscapes. They liked her painting, and her work was included in their exhibitions. This brought her recognition and respect.

In 1937, Carr had a serious heart attack. As she had to spend much time in bed, she began writing. She wrote *Klee Wyck* in 1941. The title was a name the Aboriginals called her, meaning "Laughing One." The book was a collection of pieces about themes similar to her painting—Aboriginal totems, abandoned villages, and natural scenery. Her writing was immediately successful and, to her surprise, she received the Governor General's Award. The appreciation for both her writing and her painting had come late in her life. She was seventy years old when *Klee Wyck* was released. It was translated into French in 1973. Much of her writing as well as her journals were published after she died in 1945.

Gabrielle Roy

Gabrielle Roy was born in Manitoba but settled in Montreal when the war started. There, she began working as a freelance journalist and writing her novel *Bonheur d'occasion*. It is a story about Montreal's poor at the end of the Depression. She published the novel in 1945. Roy became the first Canadian to win the Prix Fémina in Paris. She went on to win the Literary Guild of America Award in New York as well as the first of three Governor General's Awards in 1947. Her highly regarded novel was translated into 15 languages. The English version was called *The Tin Flute*. Gabrielle Roy became the first woman to become a member of the Royal Society of Canada when she was given the Lorne Pierce Medal. She continued writing novels, essays, and children's stories. She earned many awards and prizes, including the Prix Duvernay and the Molson Prize. Gabrielle Roy was also named a Companion to the Order of Canada in 1967.

Writing What He Knows

At first, Hugh MacLennan tried to write novels with international themes and topics. He was not very successful. Then, he began writing about what he knew. MacLennan decided to write about the Halifax explosion he survived when he was a boy. As an experiment he wrote *Barometer Rising*, which was published in 1941. His switch from international themes to Canadian ones brought him great success. It also welcomed a new phase of literature to Canada. This national focus was carried on in MacLennan's 1945 novel *Two Solitudes*. It is a story about the French-English problems in Quebec. Much of his writing was based in Montreal. However, it touched upon universal themes and ideas shared by the entire country. His novels won him the Governor General's Award three times, one of these awards being for *Two Solitudes*. He also won the award twice for his nonfiction writing. He won many other awards, and became the first Canadian to receive Princeton University's James Madison Medal, which is given to a graduate who has excelled in his profession.

Canadian Decades 1940s

Science and Technology

The final assembly of CF-100 jet fighters was done in a plant near Toronto, Ontario.

Aviation Advancements

The **Cold War** made the Canadian military prepare for the worst. Canada lies between two superpowers, the United States and the Soviet Union. In 1949, Canada decided to flex its muscles. The Royal Canadian Air Force showed the world how far its planes could fly. The Canadair North Star, based on a DC-4 airliner but with a Rolls Royce engine, left Vancouver on June 15. It landed in Halifax eight and a half hours later. It had completed the first non-stop coast-to-coast flight. The plane travelled 4,630 kilometres, at an average speed of 529 kilometres per hour.

In August of the same year, Avro Canada Ltd. tested a new jetliner. This four-engined jet was the first of its kind in North America, and only the second in the world. It could carry fifty passengers at an altitude of up to 9,000 metres at 692 kilometres per hour.

The plane was Canadian-built and -designed. An American equivalent had yet to be created. Avro created the CF-100 military jet fighter in 1950. It had long-range radar equipment and was an all-weather machine. This was important to ensure all of Canada could be reached by the jet fighter.

Penfield Travels the Brain

Wilder Penfield studied medicine at England's Oxford University. He was inspired by Sir Charles Sherrington, a neurophysiologist at Oxford, who studied the brain and spinal column. Penfield decided to follow in Sherrington's footsteps. For the rest of his life, he researched the brain. Many modern discoveries were drawn from Penfield's findings. His papers and handbooks became standard references for brain research.

In 1934, Penfield founded the Montreal Neurological Institute, which became an international centre for education, research, and treatment of nervous system diseases. During World War II, Penfield and his researchers studied the problems of military medicine. They looked at **fatigue** in bomber crews, brain swelling, nervous illnesses, blackouts, and healing. In 1941, he picked up Sir Frederick Banting's research into seasickness—Penfield and Charles Best found the cause and treatment for it. Penfield travelled the world studying and teaching medicine. Dr. Penfield saw the brain as the most important unexplored field in science, and he became an invaluable explorer.

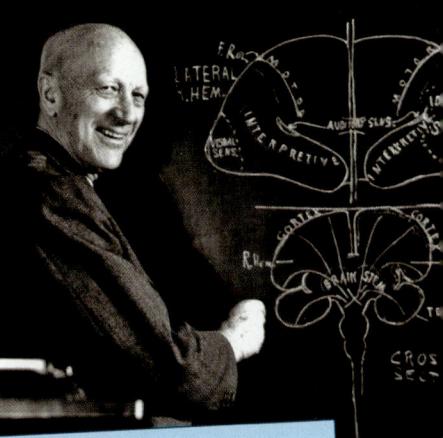

"The splitting of the atom was child's play as compared with our task of charting the mechanisms of the central nervous system, mechanisms on which thought and behaviour must depend."
—Wilder Penfield

Supplies in the Air

Carl Agar learned to fly airplanes in Edmonton. He joined the Royal Canadian Air Force in 1940 and received a medal for his success as a flight teacher. He flew the first commercial helicopter into Canada to spray orchards with insecticide in 1947. Agar pushed the limits of what helicopters could do. He developed his skills to the point where he could fly easily in mountains. He could carry out land surveys from the sky. It also gave him access to remote areas. In 1949, Agar airlifted construction materials, equipment, and workers to the Palisade Lake Dam in British Columbia. He used helicopters in a different way than was ever done before. This versatility made him very successful. His company, Okanagan Air Service, was one of the largest helicopter businesses in the world.

▎Frederick Banting also worked on finding a treatment for seasickness for naval officers in the 1940s.

Banting's Studies Cut Short

Dr. Frederick Banting was famous for his discovery of insulin in 1922. However, in 1941, he was working on military issues, including the problems of aviation medicine. Pilots often passed out when they reached certain heights. He went overseas to conduct his research and returned to Canada eager to test his ideas. Banting built a decompression chamber, a steel vessel that changed pressure levels, to measure the effects of altitude on people. He wanted to fly with the Air Force to test real situations. Banting developed a suit that he hoped would stop blackouts. He was being sent to Europe in a bomber plane to complete his tests.

As the bomber took off, it lost an engine. The plane made a forced landing in a snowstorm, killing two of the crew immediately. Banting was seriously injured. When he regained consciousness, he rapidly **dictated** medical information to the pilot. He quickly explained his theories and discoveries. He hoped that his information would help others complete his research. The pilot left in search of help, but was unsuccessful. He returned to find Banting dead. It took three days before help arrived at the wreckage.

Canadian Decades 1940s

Sports

Breaking Colour Barriers

Jackie Robinson was the first black man to play major league baseball. He joined the Montreal Royals farm team in 1946. Robinson played out his career with the Brooklyn Dodgers. The team challenged the unwritten rule banning black baseball players from playing in the major leagues, but Robinson knew that he would not be welcomed by the Dodgers' players or fans.

In 1947, Robinson played his first major league game. More than 26,500 fans came to watch. He hit his first home run in April. When he returned to the dugout, none of his teammates shook his hand. Despite this, he continued to play well. By the season's end, Robinson was ranked second to Bing Crosby as the "Most Admired Man." Two years later, Robinson and three others became the first black players to play in the all-star game. Robinson opened the door for other black baseball players to make it to the major leagues.

■ Robinson earned the respect of baseball fans and nonfans alike.

Maple Leaf Legend

Syl Apps was an Olympic pole vaulter before he joined the Toronto Maple Leafs hockey team in 1936. He was team leader in scoring and was the Rookie of the Year. He won the Lady Byng trophy for sportsmanship in 1942, and was either a first- or second-team all-star centre five times. He had seven successful seasons with the team, acting as team captain for most of his career. In 1943, Apps took a break from his hockey career to join the Canadian army. He picked up where he left off when he returned from overseas, and led the Leafs for another three years. He retired in 1948. At the end of his career, Apps had 201 goals, 432 points in 423 games. In recognition of his achievements, Syl Apps was inducted into the Hockey Hall of Fame in 1961.

▍Apps helped his team win the Stanley Cup three times before he hung up his skates.

Edmonton Grads Move On

The Commercial Graduates Basketball Club began as a women's high school team. The Grads, as they became known, dominated women's basketball from 1915 until 1940. They rarely lost a game and won 49 out of 51 titles. They won the Underwood International Championships 23 times—they had not lost it once. Among the list of the Grads' accomplishments was the French and European Championships as well as the North American Championships. By the time the team retired, there were only 48 players listed for the 25-year life of the team. The team attracted gifted athletes who stayed with the club for as long as they could. The women were more than great basketball players. They were also representatives of Edmonton. They were hailed as a Canadian institution and promoted Canada abroad. Dr. James Naismith, the inventor of basketball, called them "the finest basketball team that ever stepped out on a floor."

▍The Edmonton Grads dominated women's basketball for decades. They rarely lost games or players.

Hockey Hall Recognizes Achievement

Canada's unofficial national sport was finally officially honoured in 1943. The Hockey Hall of Fame was established to honour the excellent athletes and administrators in the game. The players, officials, and builders of hockey who made great contributions to the game were remembered in the Hall. Hockey artifacts displayed at the Hall included goalie masks, sticks, trophies, and international hockey sweaters. A selection committee of media and people who know the game chose the players elected to the Hall. The Hall of Fame also served to promote the sport in the Canadian community.

The Hockey Hall of Fame was first built at the Canadian National Exhibition (CNE) in Toronto. It was founded by the National Hockey League, the Canadian Amateur Hockey Association, and the City of Toronto. While the CNE buildings were being built, the Hall shared space with Canada's Sports Hall of Fame. It has since moved to a location in downtown Toronto.

Canadian Decades 1940s

Sports

Canada's Golden Girl

Canadians watched in awe as Barbara Ann Scott skated to the top. The 18-year-old girl from Ottawa won the World Figure Skating Championship on February 16, 1947. It was the first time a Canadian had earned the honour. She beat out 21 other skaters from seven countries to win the title. Scott was not finished yet, however. The next year, in St. Moritz, Switzerland, she became the first Canadian to win a gold medal in figure skating at the Olympic Games. She overcame ice that was rough after a hockey game, and she performed flawlessly. She out-skated 24 other women from around the world. After Barbara Ann Scott finished her routine, the fans cheered. They had picked their favourite to be the gold-medal winner even before the rest of the skaters had competed.

▌Barbara Ann Scott performed amazing moves, including a spectacular stag jump, at a competition in Stockholm.

Number Nine At Number Fifty

Maurice "The Rocket" Richard was one of the Montreal Canadiens' most loved players. After battling injuries, he scored 32 goals in his first full season. In the 1944–45 season, Richard scored 50 goals in 50 games—a record that was enthusiastically celebrated. In the last game of the season, "The Rocket" scored on the Boston Bruins, and even the Bruins fans cheered and gave him a standing ovation. The players closest to Richard in the scoring race had only 29 goals for the season. He led the league in goals five times. Despite his incredible goal-scoring ability, the Rocket never had the assists needed to clinch the league scoring title. He won the Hart Trophy for the Most Valuable Player in 1947. Many times he scored several goals in a game. Richard scored three goals in a game for a hat trick, and he scored four goals in a game twice. He scored all five goals in a 5–1 victory over Toronto in 1944. Many of his records remained unbroken until the 1980s.

▌Over the course of his career, Maurice Richard scored a total of 544 goals.

Grey Cup

In 1948, the Calgary Stampeders broke the East's hold on the Grey Cup. They met the Ottawa Rough Riders in the big game and won. This was not an ordinary year, however. For the first time, the Grey Cup final was not just a football game. It now involved a festival that lasted for a week before the contest. It had become a national celebration. Calgary fans' enthusiasm spread. The Stampeders' logo was a horse, and the fan club brought a dozen horses to Toronto. They rode a horse through the Royal York Hotel in downtown Toronto. Aboriginal chiefs attended in full traditional costume. There were chuckwagons shipped out by train. The Stampeders' supporters served pancake breakfasts from the back of them. Calgary fans brought the West to the East and came home victorious. The Grey Cup was the most watched sporting event in the country.

Johnny the Jockey Wins Triple Crown

John Longden's career lasted 40 years and was crammed with achievements. He won more than 6,000 horse races. Only 10 other jockeys in history have enjoyed that many victories. Longden and his family lived near Taber, Alberta, where he worked in the coal mines during the week and raced horses on the weekend. He visited Salt Lake City, Utah, in 1927, and won a race on a horse named Hugo K. Asher. That began his successful career as a jockey.

Longden trained and rode a horse called Count Fleet. In the 1930s and early 1940s, Longden won three Louisiana Derby races. In 1943, he won the Kentucky Derby, Preakness, and Belmont Stakes with Count Fleet, thus riding the horse to a Triple Crown victory. These accomplishments earned him a spot in the National Museum of Racing's Hall of Fame in New York. After retiring, John Longden trained horses. His most famous horse was Majestic Prince, which went on to win the Kentucky Derby.

▮ Johnny Longden earned a place in horse racing history. He and his horse, Count Fleet, won several races across North America.

WORLD FOCUS

Joe DiMaggio American Hero

"Jolting" Joe DiMaggio was the greatest outfielder ever to play the game. People thought he was good enough to replace Babe Ruth when he entered spring training in 1936. He did not disappoint. He played professional baseball for 13 seasons. His style of play was smooth and easy, both in the field and at the plate. He had great statistics, and he hit 28 home runs a year despite battling injuries. DiMaggio owned the Yankee's outfield, and no one ever doubted that. In 1941, Joe DiMaggio had a 56-game hitting streak, and finished the season with 30 home runs and 125 runs batted in. He also had pride in his country. He took a three-year break in 1943 in order to fight in the war.

Joe DiMaggio tested the imagination of American baseball fans as well as those who never watched the game. DiMaggio was somewhat of a mystery. He did not speak openly with the press, so details about his personal life were not easy to come by. He married silver-screen goddess Marilyn Monroe in 1954. She was a woman about whom every man dreamed and who every woman envied. They divorced later that year. Songs and books in the 1960s and 1970s spoke of the impact Joe DiMaggio had on the United States. He remains an American sports legend even after his death in 1999.

▮ DiMaggio's 56-game hitting streak in 1941 is one of the most respected records in history.

Canadian Decades 1940s   31

Economy

Social Welfare Introduced

No one wanted Canada to experience the suffering it had during the 1930s' Great Depression. To prevent this from happening, the government created a safety net for the poor. In 1943, The Unemployment Insurance Act called for social security through family allowance and health coverage. Also, Saskatchewan's hospital plan of 1945 covered every provincial resident. Its success caused other provinces to follow its lead.

In the same year, the government offered the provinces a grant for the development of medical and hospital insurance. The government also suggested old-age pensions for Canadians over the age of 70, and a cost-shared pension for people between 65 and 69 years old. The government was to take responsibility for the unemployed. Arguments between the provincial and federal governments over how to share the cost could not be solved. The plans were put on hold. In 1951, universal old-age pensions were brought into effect.

Canada Booms as Allies Bomb

Industry in Canada took off during the war. European and Asian countries were not strong economically. This opened more markets to which Canadian manufacturers could sell. After the war, industry was switched to peacetime products. New homes were built as quickly as post-war material shortages would allow. There were many new families, which created great demand in many industries.

However, the boom had a cost, too. The demand for goods and a population increase because of immigration caused an increase in imports of U.S. goods. Canadian exports, which had been to Europe before the war, decreased. Canada grew more dependent on the United States to meet its citizens' demands. By 1950, the economies in Europe had recovered, and these problems disappeared. Canada's economic boom continued.

▎Canada produced weapons and military equipment for the Allies.

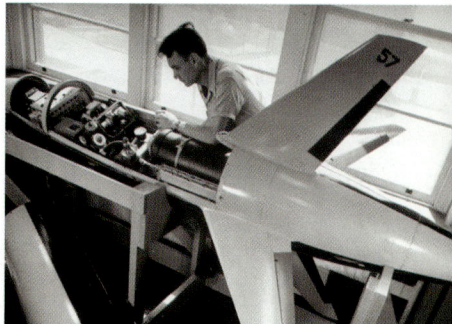

Gatt Established

In 1947, 22 countries signed the General Agreement on **Tariffs** and Trade (GATT). The organization aimed to free up how countries traded with each other. Each country had to give other member countries the same deals on tariffs as it gave to its best trading partner. Canada negotiated with seven of the member countries. The talks between Canada and the United States were the most intensive. The 1930s agreements between the two neighbours were replaced by GATT conditions.

The rules were clear, but there were exceptions. Preferences that existed before GATT could be kept in place. Canada kept the trade benefits it received from the Britain Commonwealth preferences. Some exceptions, however, were against Canada's interests. Agricultural products were not included in the trade agreement. Canada and other agricultural exporters objected.

Canadians Look After Families

In 1945, the government began a family allowance program, which included a "baby bonus" to every family. This allotted money for each child to make sure he or she was cared for. The money was intended to help families pay for medical and dental expenses, food, and housing for children under 16 years old. This applied to all families in the country, including wealthy families that did not need the help. Families that made more money were taxed on the family allowance assistance. They also received only a percentage of the possible amount. The government gave lower-income families $5 a month for each child under six and $8 for a child between 13 and 15. The program cost $250 million to operate during the first year alone.

▎Before the Leduc oil find, Albertans had counted on the Turner Valley oil field for income. This new field led to more oil and more money for Canadian oil companies.

Alberta Strikes Black Gold

In 1947, oil was discovered in Leduc, Alberta. The Leduc field was larger than the nearly spent one in Turner Valley. In the following years, even bigger oil fields were discovered. Exploration in Alberta, Saskatchewan, and Manitoba unearthed new oil and gas reserves. The oil boom led to growth in other industries as well. Drilling required that plants and pipelines be built. Canada was now able to support its own energy needs.

Canadian Decades 1940s 33

Fashion

Models in glamour magazines showed off the latest fashions in exotic locations. Meanwhile, Canada and Europe had to live on war rations.

Fashion Magazines

American magazines such as *Vogue* and *Harper's Bazaar* were glossy magazines. A new, confident style of dressing was splashed on every page. The models were less posed in the 1940s, giving a more casual look to the photographs. The pages were in full colour, and vacation clothes were shown at holiday sites. The articles encouraged people to travel around the world. The magazines seemed not to be aware that the world was at war.

Resort clothes were colourful. Men wore casual pants and Hawaiian print shirts. People read these magazines and tried to copy what they saw. As North America became involved in the war, it was more difficult to dress like magazine models or movie stars. America and Canada soon felt the fashion crunch of rationing and restrictions.

Politicians Dictate War Designs

Before the war got under way, designers continued to create fashion for people not very affected by the war. By 1940, France, the centre of fashion design, had fallen to Germany. Now, the war affected all parts of life in all parts of the world, even fashion.

Shortages in materials and labour changed the face of fashion. What people wore was now not just a personal choice. The government had a say in it. What clothes were made of, how they were made, and what they cost was a federal concern. This had never happened before. The restrictions applied to everyone across the board, regardless of how much money he or she had or what he or she did for a living. In many places, clothes were rationed. The amount of cloth used to make clothes was limited. Even trimmings such as lace and ribbon were cut back.

From Men's Wear Back to Women's

Women dressed much like men in the early 1940s. Men's suits were shapeless and boxy. Women wore these boxy jackets and utility pants to work. Utility skirts were plain and fell just below the knee. They did not show off a woman's figure, but they served a purpose. Once the war was over, designers began creating styles for women's bodies again. Longer skirts and fitted waist bands were the style in 1947. What was called the "New Look" consisted of soft, flowing dresses and tailored jackets. They were a "must" in any woman's wardrobe. Dressy clothes once again became more common.

Men's fashion also changed at the end of the war. Soldiers returning from the war often did not have suitable clothing to wear. Many were boys when they left, and their bodies had since changed. As the troops were **demobilized**, the soldiers were given civilian suits to wear—a tie, shirt, shoes, and raincoat.

Many people did not like the suits, saying the clothes were of poor quality and were too boxy to be stylish. Regardless, men continued to wear what were called "demob suits," short for "demobilization," for many years after the war.

▌"Demob" suits were made by several companies and were sent to different demobilization centres. People could tell where a soldier had been demobilized by the type of suit he was given.

▌Berets of the 1940s were made of felt and were worn at a tilted angle.

Fads

Headwear was popular in the 1940s. During the war, women wore enlarged berets, which were inspired by military uniforms. Women also wore scarves, either in a turban style tied at the front, tied under the chin, or around the neck. Later, pill-box hats and other small hats became trendy. These were worn at the back of the head and were much less overpowering than the larger, pre-war styles.

In contrast to women's fads, men rarely wore hats after the war. The focus for them was their hair styles. While hair was still short at the back, men began experimenting with how it was cut at the front, from flat tops or crew cuts to longer hair that was allowed to curl.

Canadian Decades 1940s 35

Immigration

▍Many people felt that the Jewish children would not have become orphaned if the Canadian government had allowed more Jewish immigration before the war.

Jewish Orphans Accepted Too Late

In 1947, the Canadian government opened the country to 1,000 Jewish orphans, who had lost their parents in concentration camps or in fighting in Europe. Some Canadians felt that this helping hand had come too late. As Adolf Hitler rose in power before the war started, Jewish people in Poland and other European countries became afraid for their lives. Hitler spoke about ridding the world of Jewish people, and the Jews wanted to leave before Hitler acted on his hate. Many Jewish people asked for permission to immigrate to Canada to escape what they felt was sure to come. They were denied. There were only a few immigrants who were able to get through the Canadian restrictions. Like many other Western countries, Canada was not sympathetic to the Jews' situation until after the war. Had policy-makers responded to the Jewish call for help in the early 1940s, many innocent lives might have been saved.

36 Immigration

Policy Changes Increase Immigration

After the war, many Europeans were without homes. Canada agreed to accept 10,000 displaced people, and then it upped the number to 20,000. Cabinet members visited Europe in 1947. They saw the devastation first-hand. They said there were many camps housing citizens who had lost their homes in Austria and Germany. Some of these people could be acceptable Canadians. The government representatives also said that the number might again increase, depending on the outcome of international talks.

Allowing immigrants into Canada enriched the immigrants' life, but it was a mutual relationship. Large numbers of immigrants served Canadian purposes as well. The economic boom enjoyed during the war created a demand for labour. Thousands of people were admitted to Canada who would have previously been considered undesirable. They contributed to the workforce pool for Canadian businesses and industry.

Immigrant Explosion

Throughout the 1940s, the number of immigrants Canada accepted drastically increased. There was also a huge difference between the number of women and the number of men seeking to become Canadian citizens in some years. One reason for this was that after the war, many women came to Canada as war brides, and relaxed immigration laws allowed families to be reunited.

YEAR	MEN	WOMEN
1940	5,371	5,953
1941	4,791	4,538
1942	3,208	4,368
1943	3,290	5,214
1944	4,494	8,307
1945	7,701	15,021
1946	20,483	51,236
1947	33,435	30,692
1948	67,090	58,324
1949	51,162	44,055

Family ties

Immigration restrictions were further relaxed in the 1940s. The Canadian government allowed entry to immigrants who had family already living in Canada. The number of immigrants coming to live in Canada skyrocketed. Around 500,000 people entered the country from Italy and Greece alone to become citizens. These families had kept close ties with each other even though they lived oceans apart. When the policy amendment was announced, extended families were notified, and thousands flocked to Canada to take advantage of the change.

Canadian Citizens First

Before 1947, people who had come from Britain and started families in Canada were considered Britons living elsewhere. The Canadian Citizenship Act was passed in 1947. It was the first legislation to classify people as Canadians. The Act stated that a woman did not lose her nationality through marriage. Before the Act, women who became Canadian through marriage could lose their citizenship if the marriage broke up. Now, women were Canadian despite the outcome of the relationship. The children of these people were also Canadian citizens first—they were not British citizens born away from Britain. The Citizenship Act stated that whether a person was born in Canada, married a Canadian, or was an immigrant, he or she was given the same rights as other Canadians.

▌Prime Minister W. L. Mackenzie King was the first Canadian to receive a citizenship certificate under the 1947 act.

Music and the Arts

> "When we played for the Forces during the war, we brought a piece of each man's home town into each camp we visited."
> —Mart Kenney

Big Band Swing

Mart Kenney and His Western Gentlemen formed in the thirties. They appeared across the country, touring hotel ballrooms and large clubs. They often entertained at the prestigious Royal York Hotel in Toronto, but they never forgot about the small towns along the way. The Gentlemen were heard every Sunday on CBC radio and also aired on British and American stations. When the war hit, the band tried to enlist as entertainers. They were denied. To do their part, Mart Kenney and his band travelled to army camps to entertain troops. They performed at Victory Bond Shows aimed at raising money for the war effort. Mart Kenney and the Western Gentlemen were named the favourite Canadian orchestra by *Orchestra World* magazine, and they were named *Liberty Magazine*'s Band of the Year in 1948. The big band swing of Mart Kenney, with various bands behind him, played on well into the nineties.

▌Mart Kenney and His Western Gentlemen were Canada's leading dance band in the 1930s and 1940s.

■ Bing Crosby sang what many soldiers were feeling in "White Christmas." Canadian songwriters also contributed to the patriotic songs of World War II.

Patriotic Songs

Before the war, people listened to and sang such songs as "Over the Rainbow," "Tuxedo Junction," and "Honeysuckle Rose." These ditties were soon replaced by patriotic songs and songs about the war. Bing Crosby's classic "White Christmas" was first sung in 1942 and expressed the soldiers' dream to be at home with their families during the holidays. There were also songs released that were intended to boost morale and support for Canadian soldiers at home. These songs included "The White Cliffs of Dover," "Praise the Lord and Pass the Ammunition," and "There'll Always Be an England." At the end of the war, music returned to its previous style. In 1946, for example, the war theme in music had been dropped, and bands from coast to coast played light-hearted songs, such as "Zip-a-Dee-Doo-Dah."

Guy Lombardo and the Royal Canadians

Talking about the Big Band era would not be complete without Guy Lombardo. His dance band, The Royal Canadians, was one of the most popular in North America. They formed in 1916 and played well into the 1960s. They sold more than 300 million records in the 50 years they performed together. They produced about 500 hit songs. Guy Lombardo was responsible for introducing Canadian and American society to the phrase "sweetest music this side of heaven." Guy Lombardo and The Royal Canadians were named the top of the pops for 10 straight years. The band was best known for its New Year's Eve radio broadcasts from New York, during which they played their theme "Auld Lang Syne." The song is still sung at the stroke of midnight on December 31 across North America.

■ Lombardo's New Year's Eve Party became the longest running annual special broadcast in radio history.

WORLD FOCUS

Old Blue Eyes, Frank Sinatra, Croons His Way to the Top

Big Band leader Harry James went to a club to find a singer he had heard on the radio. The club manager said the band did not have a singer, but a waiter acted as emcee and sang sometimes. James immediately asked the young man to join his band. The singing waiter was Frank Sinatra.

In 1939, Sinatra recorded "All or Nothing at All," but it did not become a hit until 1943. A musicians' strike in 1941 caused a recording ban. Singers were not members of the union, so could continue to perform. With the focus away from the famous band leaders, vocalists including Sinatra became stars on their own. By 1942, "Old Blue Eyes" recorded his first records under his own rather than a band's name. He was a phenomenon. Women screamed with excitement when Sinatra came on the stage, and his romantic ballads had them buying his records faster than he could produce them. His wild success continued throughout the decade. Sinatra's music, as well as his movies, kept him in the spotlight until his death in 1998 at the age of 82.

Canadian Decades 1940s   39

Society

During World War II, women served in a variety of non-combat roles, such as radar operators, ambulance drivers, and mechanics.

The New Look of the Military

Prior to World War II, women's roles in the military were limited to nursing. By 1945, the number of medical corps nurses serving in the war had reached 4,480. However, during the war, there was a shortage of men to fight. The British had added women to their forces, and Canada followed their example. The Canadian Women's Army Corps and the Royal Canadian Air Force (Women's Division) were formed in 1941, and the Royal Canadian Naval Women's Service was established the following year. The number of women joining the wartime forces climbed to 45,423. They worked in clerical, administrative, communications, and other support positions. These jobs had been done by men, who were now freed up for active duty. Their contribution to the war effort was great. However, after the war ended, the three women's services were cancelled. This, again, left only nurses in uniform. It was not until 1951 that the forces grew, and women were again recruited.

Support the War—Save, Ration, and Invest!

The government encouraged people to invest in Victory Bonds and War Savings Certificates to help support the war. The bonds helped the government finance the war and were sold to all Canadians, even children. Young people were encouraged to buy stamps with planes or tanks on them for a quarter. Their parents planted gardens on unused patches of land so that less food would have to be brought in. They donated pots and pans to be melted down for weapons. They were asked to conserve energy as best they could—dress in warm layers instead of burning more fuel.

Canadians' food was rationed. Meat, sugar, tea, and coffee were among the items that were carefully watched. Gasoline, aluminum, and metal goods were also restricted. To save gas, drivers were asked to obey a speed limit of 40 kilometres per hour. Very few people followed the law. New cars or new tires were impossible to buy, as the metal and rubber was being used for war products. Even everyday items such as hairpins were difficult to find. Citizens did all they could to support "their boys" fighting in Europe, Asia, and Africa.

▎Posters were designed to encourage Canadians to support the war from home.

Military Marriages

The end of the war signalled the beginning of married life for many Canadian servicemen. One in five bachelors sent to Europe to fight got married in the process. In 1946, more than 47,000 European brides and more than 21,000 small children boarded ships bound for their new home—Canada. Most of these women were British. A Canadian Wives' Bureau was set up in London, England, to offer advice about life in Canada. Many war brides were not ready for the differences between Europe and Canada. They had to adjust to a new way of life.

The government was supportive of its military men. The country paid for the brides' sea and rail travel to get them to their husbands. They were given food allowances and access to medical care on the boats and trains.

Women Workers

When World War II began, men went off to fight, but life continued at home. Industries had to produce goods that would support the war, such as weapons. Single women were asked to replace their brothers in the workplace. They were doing the same jobs as men, but for much lower wages. As the war raged on, more men were sent overseas. Industry at home needed more workers. The government offered tax breaks and daycare services to draw married women into the labour force. When the war ended, these incentives to work were taken away. Women were encouraged to give up their jobs to the returning men. Sometimes, laws were passed that forced the women out of their positions. Many women chose to stay in the workforce, and they entered the growing number of "female" jobs in service industries.

Canadian Decades 1940s   41

Canada/U.S. Relations

Allies in War

The American and Canadian forces came together during the Rhineland Campaign in February 1945. The Canadian army attacked from the south, and the Americans pushed in from the north. The two came together in the area around the Rhine, a river in Germany. The mission was not easy, but together the North Americans were successful. They were assisted by British forces as they cleared the Germans away from their last strong line of defence. This victory led to the final campaign in Northwest Europe. It took the Allied forces across the Rhine and farther into Germany. The cooperation between the United States and Canada, along with the rest of the Allied forces, helped bring the war to an end.

▌Following their victory on the beaches of Normandy, the Allies began their advance toward Germany.

The Atomic Age

Prime Minister King and American President Harry Truman joined forces with Britain's Prime Minister Clement Attlee in 1945. They met in Washington, D.C., to discuss what to do about atomic weapons. The three countries were considered the atomic powers, as they were the main participants in dropping the atomic bomb on Japan. The leaders agreed to share their knowledge of atomic power, but there were concerns and conditions. They would talk about atomic weapons as long as the other countries guaranteed that such weapons would not be used in war. King, Truman, and Attlee all agreed that, if countries developed atomic weapons, it would be extremely dangerous for everyone. The leaders hoped that nations would obey the international laws and avoid war in the future. They also encouraged countries to support the new United Nations organization.

▎British, U.S., and Canadian leaders met at the White House in Washington, D.C. to discuss the atomic weapons situation.

American Heroes

The United States joined the war in 1941. Canadians admired the strength of their southern neighbours, and polls showed that many Canadians would have liked to join the U.S. This new feeling toward the Americans worried Prime Minister King. Despite King's feelings, Canada kept a close relationship with the United States. It even expanded its defence and other relations with the United States after the war. The two countries went on to sign many agreements that aimed at securing North American borders. This was more important because of the Cold War building between the United States and the Soviet Union. These pacts included NORAD, which was a joint air defence pact signed in 1958.

Hyde Park Agreement

Before the United States officially joined the war, Canada had already begun expanding its industries. It bought a great deal of equipment and machinery from the U.S. By 1941, Canada was running low on its exchange reserves of American money. It turned to the United States for help. Prime Minister King and President Roosevelt came to the Hyde Park Agreement later that year. This agreement allowed for greater U.S. purchases in Canada, and for Britain to use military supplies imported into Canada from the U.S. These conditions eased the cash problem Canada was experiencing. Canada could now cover its imports from the United States. Any agreement bonding the U.S. and Canada was highly supported by Canadians.

North American Defence

In 1938, the world was bracing for an international conflict. American President Franklin D. Roosevelt promised to protect Canada if it was threatened during a war. In 1940, after two days of negotiations, the Ogdensburg Agreement was reached. It created a Permanent Joint Board of Defence for North America. It addressed issues such as delivering weapons from American factories to Canadian forces. The agreement also rested on a free exchange of defence information. If Germany or Japan attacked North America, the agreement stated that both sides would defend the coasts and make use of airfields. This agreement signalled a shift in Canada's alliance. Canada realized a common interest in ideals and geography that it shared with the United States. This commonality was no longer present with Great Britain.

▎President Roosevelt and Prime Minister King signed the Ogdensburg Agreement in Ogdensburg, New York, on August 17, 1940.

Activities

Where did it happen?

Match the event to the place in Canada where it happened.

a) Japanese Canadians forced to leave the area
b) Oil is discovered
c) Polio research is carried out
d) Thomas Douglas's home capital
e) Joined confederation in 1949
f) Jackie Robinson's first team
g) St. Roch's journey
h) Train crash site
i) Where the spy drama unfolded
j) Where the North Star landed

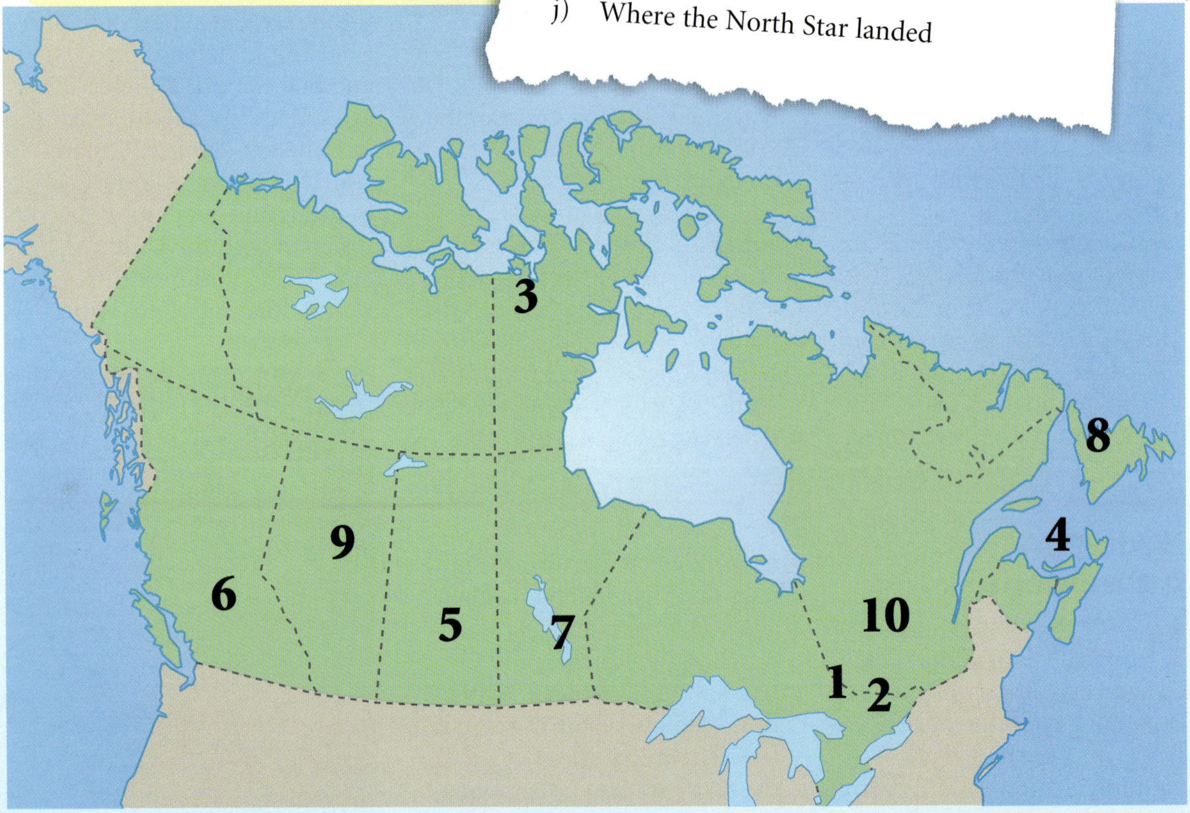

Answers:
1. i; 2. c; 3. g; 4. j; 5. d; 6. a; 7. h; 8. e; 9. b; 10. f.

44   Activities

Newsmakers

Match the person in the news with his or her story!

a) exposed a spy ring
b) brought independence to Israel
c) dance band leader
d) studied the science of the brain
e) introduced social security
f) convinced Newfoundland to join Canada
g) used a helicopter to ship supplies to remote areas
h) was the first Social Credit leader
i) was a Hollywood film success
j) first Canadian to win Prix Fémina

1. Prime Minister King
2. Wilder Penfield
3. Carl Agar
4. William Aberhart
5. Igor Gouzenko
6. Deanna Durbin
7. David Ben-Gurion
8. Mart Kenney
9. Gabrielle Roy
10. Joseph Smallwood

Answers: 1. e; 2. d; 3. g; 4. h; 5. a; 6. i; 7. b; 8. c; 9. j; 10. f.

True or False

1. A vaccine for polio was found by a Canadian.
2. NATO was Canada's first peacetime military alliance.
3. Quebec was the first province to give women the right to vote in province elections.
4. Canadians could not buy a new car during most of the war.
5. Frederick Banting was able to pass on some of his research ideas before he died.

Answers:
1. F (Dr. Salk was American, but the research company responsible for making large quantities of the vaccine was Canadian)
2. T
3. F (It was the last province to give women this privilege.)
4. T
5. T

Canadian Decades 1940s 45

Glossary

advocate: a person who speaks in favour of something or someone

Allies: the military group fighting the Axis powers; included Great Britain, France, Canada, and the United States

arsonist: a person who intentionally sets fires

autobiographical: a story written about oneself by oneself

Axis powers: the military group fighting together, consisting of Germany, Japan, and Italy

Cold War: tensions between the two superpowers the United States and the Soviet Union

collective security: a guarantee by a group of countries of the safety of each country, and the maintenance of peace through group action

commandants: officers in command of bases or camps

communism: an economic and social system in which property and goods are owned by the government and shared by citizens

concentration camps: prison camps where political enemies, prisoners of war, and interned foreigners are held

conscription: a law that requires enlistment into the military

correspondents: people who gather news in a distant place and send it home

defected: left one's own country for another for political or social reasons

demobilized: disbanded after the war

democracy: a government that is run by people through elected leaders

dictated: said or read something aloud for another person to write down

espionage: the use of spies by one country to discover military secrets of another

fasted: voluntarily went without food, usually for a cause

fatigue: physical or mental weariness

Holocaust: the systematic killing of more than 6 million Jews by the Nazis in World War II

insulin: a treatment for diabetes, it allows the body to use sugar and other carbohydrates

interned: forcibly confined within a country or place, especially during a war

newsreels: short films dealing with current events

patriotic: having pride and love for one's country

propaganda: the spread of beliefs and opinions, often by deception and stretching the facts

sabotage: destruction or damage done in order to hurt or harm someone

socialist: one who believes in socialism—the means of production and distribution should be owned, managed, or controlled by a central, elected body or government and not by individuals

stereotypical: an overly simple vision of a person or group, usually not based on facts

stronghold: a secure place or centre; a fort or fortress

tariffs: duty or tax on goods

vaccine: a medicine made from a weakened virus of a given disease that is used to protect people against that disease

vaudeville: a show consisting of a variety of acts, including singing, dancing, juggling, short plays, and animal acts

virus: tiny particles that enter the body and carry disease and illness